IYAD HAYATLEH is a Palestinian poet grew up in Syria. He has lived in G part in many cultural events and t. He has given many readings in the UK including the Edinburgh International Book Festival. He has published some of his poems in magazines and collective poetry books in Scotland in both languages, Arabic and English, and had his first collection published by Survivors' Press, called *Beyond all measure*, in 2007.

TESSA RANSFORD (www.wisdomfield.com) is an established poet, translator, literary editor and cultural activist on many fronts over the last 40 years, having also worked as founder and director of the Scottish Poetry Library.

Tessa initiated the annual Callum Macdonald Memorial Award for publishers of pamphlet poetry in Scotland, now in its twelfth year, with the attendant fairs and website: www.scottish-pamphlet-poetry.com. She has had Royal Literary Fund fellowships at the Centre for Human Ecology and Queen Margaret University. She was president of Scottish PEN from 2003–6.

Tessa's *Not Just Moonshine, New and Selected Poems* was published in 2008 by Luath Press, Edinburgh and a new book of poems: *don't mention this to anyone*, in 2012.

إياد حياتله شاعر ومترجم فلسطيني وُلد ونشأ في سوريا. يعيش في غلاسكو منذ العــام 2000، وقد شارك في العديد من الفعاليّات الثقافيّة وورشات الترجمة والشعر وقدّم أمسيات شعرية كثيرة في بريطانيا من ضمنها مشاركات في مهرجان أدنبرة الدولي للكتاب. وقد نُشرت بعض قصائده في المجلّات وكتب الشعر الجماعية في أسكوتلندا بــاللغتين العربيّــة والإنكليزيّــة، وصـدرت مجموعته الأولى عن 'سيرفايفرز برس' بعنوان "لا حدود لغربتي" في العام 2007.

تيسّا رانسفورد (www.wisdomfield.com) شاعرةٌ مرموقة ومترجمة ومحـــرّرة أدبيــــة وناشطة ثقافيّة على عدّة جبهات خلال الأربعين سنة الماضية، بالإضافة إلى أنّها أسّست مكتبــة الشعر الأسكوتلندي وعملت مديرة لها.
تيسّا أوجدت جائزة الذكرى السنويّة لكالوم ماكدونالد لناشري كتيّبات الشعر في أسكوتلندا. والتي هي الآن في سنتها الثانية عشرة، مع المعارض المرافقة لها وموقعها التالي على شبكة الإنترنت:
www.scottish-pamphlet-poetry.com .
وكانت الشاعرة قد حصلت على زمالات الصندوق الأدبي الملكي في مركز علم البيئة البشــريّة وجامعة الملكة مارغريت. وكانت رئيسة للقلم الأسكوتلندي بين عامي 2003 – 2006.
وقد نشرت لها 'لُوث برس' في أدنبرة ديوانها "ليس مجرّد ضوء قمر، قصائد جديدة ومختــارة" عام 2008، ومجموعتها الشعريّة الجديدة "لا تذكر ذلك لأحد" عام 2012.

A Rug of a Thousand Colours

Poems inspired by the Five Pillars of Islam
by two contemporary Scottish writers
each also translating the other

Iyad Hayatleh and Tessa Ransford

سجّادة من ألف لون

قصائد مستوحاة من أركان الإسلام الخمسة
لشاعرين أسكوتلنديين معاصرين
مع ترجمات متبادلة

إياد حياتله و تيسّا رانسفورد

Luath Press Limited
EDINBURGH
www.luath.co.uk

First published 2012
Reprinted 2013
Reprinted 2015
Reprinted 2019

ISBN: 978-1-908373-24-3

The paper used in this book is recyclable. It is made
from low chlorine pulps produced in a low energy, low emissions
manner from renewable forests.

Typeset in 10.5 point Sabon by
3btype.com

The authors' right to be identified as author of this work under the
Copyright, Designs and Patents Act 1988 has been asserted.

© Iyad Hayatleh and Tessa Ransford

Printed by Bell and Bain Ltd, Glasgow

نُشِر لأوّل مرّة في العام 2012

الرقم القياسي الدوّلي للكتاب
ISBN: 978-1-908373-24-3

الورق المستخدم في هذا الكتاب من النوع القابل لإعادة التصنيع، وقد صُنع
من العجائن الورقيّة المنخفضة الكلور والمنتجة بطريقة الطاقة المنخفضة والإنبعاثات المنخفضة
من الغابات المتجدّدة

تمّت الطباعة بخط سابون درجة 10.5 بواسطة
3btype.com

وقد تمّ التأكيد على الإعتراف بحقوق المؤلّفين إياد حياتله وتيسّا رانسفورد
كمؤلّفين لهذا العمل وفق قانون حقوق الطبع والتصميم
وبراءات الإختراع لعام 1988

Contents

Acknowledgements	شكر وتقدير	6
Here	هُنا	8
Foreword by David Finkelstein	مقدَمة	10
Introduction by Tessa Ransford	تمهيد	12
Introduction by Iyad Hayatleh	تمهيد	20
Fifty	خَمسون	26

THE FIVE PILLARS OF ISLAM	أركان الإسلام الخمسة	
Shahada (Testimony)	شهادة	36
Testimony	شهادة	42
Salah (Prayer)	صلاة	46
Prayer-sequence	سلسلة الصلاة	50
Zakat (Almsgiving)	زكاة	58
Almsgiving	زكاة	62
Siyam (Fasting)	صِيام	66
Fasting	صِيام	70
Hajj (Pilgrimage)	حَج	72
Pilgrimage	حَج	76
Afterword by Carole Hillenbrand	خاتِمة	82

Acknowledgements

WE WISH TO THANK Creative Scotland for a grant towards the creation of this work and the following people for their help and support:

A.C. Clarke, Osama Hayatleh, Mike Knowles, Michael Lister, Lamees Tayyem, Eric Wishart.

Some of these poems have been previously published in *Gutter* magazine and on the blog, www.goldpoetrythread.blogspot.com

شكر وتقدير

نودّ أن نشكر كريتيف سكوتلاند على المنحة المقدّمة لأجل كتابة هذا العمل، أيضا نشكر هؤلاء الأشخاص على مساعدتهم ودعمهم:
إي سي كلارك، أسامة حياتله، مايك نويلز، مايكل ليستر، لميس تيّم، إيريك ويشارت

نُشرت بعض هذه القصائد سابقاً في مجلّة غتَر وفي مدوّنة غولدن بويتري ثريد

http://www.goldpoetrythread.blogspot.com

Here

in the mosques of the land of frost
I met people who came from all over the world.
Like a rug of a thousand colours…

هُنا
في مساجدِ أرض الصّقيعِ
التقيتُ أناساً أتوا مِن جميعِ الجهاتِ
كَسجّادةٍ لَونُها ألفُ لونٍ...

Foreword

MANY YEARS AGO, Robert Frost dismissively stated that 'poetry is what gets lost in translation'. The collection you hold in your hands here suggests quite the opposite.

Here we see poetry enriched by translation: a reshaping and accommodation by two accomplished writers of distinctive cultural traditions of sounds and imagery. This work marks a point of meeting, an exchange of values across a linguistic turnstile, as Tessa Ransford terms it. Translation is a complex business: it requires time, intuition and a sensitive facility with words. It involves patient negotiation as metaphoric language, verbal sounds and visual imagery are parsed and reassembled for different audiences.

A purposeful act of translation, as we see happening here, involves acts of transaction and exchange. Underpinning this compact collection of poems is an extended encounter between Tessa Ransford and Iyad Hayatleh. As Tessa points out in her introduction, the act of translation between the two involved negotiating verbal and visual differences, accommodating oral and textual understanding, finding commonality between English and Arabic expression. It was an exchange that resulted in sensitive work exploring the values, acts and emotions that make us human. Tessa and Iyad speak of love, loss, kinship, spirituality and the search for self. These are poems that move between borders, between space and time, that carry us on pilgrimages both past and present, that examine the spiritual and the physical in both deistic and humanist terms.

The poetry you find here draws us into worlds of dual perspectives and contrasts. The Arabic and English exchanges open our eyes to the porousness of text and the ability to share artistic visions between two cultures. It is a valuable point of meeting between two ways of thinking about the world. But as the selection contained here demonstrates, common to both are shared assumptions about the power of belief, the beauty of new life, the emotional grip of loss, and a continued hope for a better future. Take the time to read and savour these words.

David Finkelstein
Dean of the School of Humanities
University of Dundee

مقدّمة

ديفيد فينكلستاين
أستاذ البحوث في ثقافة وسائل الإعلام والطباعة
جامعة الملكة مارغريت، أدنبره
ترجمة إياد حياتله

قبل سنواتٍ عديدة، قال روبرت فروست مستنكراً: "الشعر هو ما يضيع في الترجمة"، ولكن هذه المجموعة التي يديكم توحي بالعكس تماماً.

هنا نرى أنّ الترجمة تُعنى بإعادة تشكيله وموضعته بين إثنين من الشعراء الضليعين ينتميان إلى تقاليد ثقافيّة متميّزة بالصوت والصورة. هذا العمل يمثّل نقطة التقاء وتبادل للقيم عبر الباب اللغوي الدوّار، كما تسمّيه تيسّا رانسفورد. الترجمة عملٌ معقّد: يتطلّب الوقت والبديهة والبراعة ذات الحساسيّة للكلمات. إنّها تستلزم الحوار الصبور كلغةٍ مجازيّة، حيث يتمّ تحليل وإعادة تركيب الأصوات اللفظيّة والصور المرئيّة لأجل جمهور مختلف.

الفعل الهادف للترجمة الذي نراه يتحقّق هنا، يشمل التعامل والتبادل. أساس هذه المجموعة المدمجة من القصائد هو مواجهة موسّعة بين تيسّا رانسفورد وإياد حياتله، وكما أشارت تيسّا في مقدّمتها، فإنّ فعل الترجمة بين الإثنين يتطلّب التفاوض على الخلافات اللفظيّة والبصريّة والتوفيق بين التفاهم الشفهي والكتابي، وإيجاد القواسم المشتركة بين التعابير الإنكليزيّة والعربيّة.

لقد كان تبادلاً أدّى إلى هذا العمل الحسّاس مستكشفا القيم والأفعال والعواطف التي تجعلنا بشراً. تيسّا وإياد يتحدثان عن الحب والخسارة، القرابة والروحانيّة والبحث عن الذات. هذه هي القصائد التي تنتقّل بين الحدود، بين الزمان والمكان، التي تحملنا في رحلة حج بين الماضي والحاضر، والتي تمتحن الروحاني والمادي في العلاقات المتبادلة بين الربوبي والإنساني.

الشعر الذي تجدونه هنا يشدّنا إلى عوالم من المناظير المزدوجة والتناقضات. التبادل بين العربيّة والإنكليزيّة يفتح أعيننا على نفاذيّة النص وقدرته على تشارك الرؤى الفنيّة بين ثقافتين. إنّه موضعٌ ثمين لإلتقاء طريقتي تفكير مختلفتين حول العالم.

Introduction

IT WAS THROUGH Iyad Hayatleh's involvement with Survivors' Poetry Scotland, a group set up by poet Gerry Loose, to publish work of people who had suffered some form of trauma, that Iyad and I first met. A Palestinian from Syria who was seeking asylum in Scotland, Iyad applied to join Scottish PEN and was accepted as a member in 2003, when he began to be involved in events. When I succeeded Simon Berry to the presidency of Scottish PEN in 2003, Simon and I set up a new committee for Writers in Exile. The result has been a fruitful series of translation workshops, small publications and events with Scottish writers and immigrant writers from various countries, mainly organised and facilitated by poet A.C. Clarke in conjunction with the group 'Artists in Exile, Glasgow'. Through this group, Iyad translated four of my poems into Arabic and I translated four of his poems into English.

After Iyad received British citizenship, he and I proposed a more major collaborative project to explore our respective cultures and religious beliefs. We decided to take the headings of the Five Pillars of Islam and to write poems inspired by these, translating one another's, open to what we might learnt in the process, with the aim of the mutual furtherance of integration, understanding and friendship. The Five Pillars are Shahada (Testimony), Salah (Prayer – at five separate times of day), Zakat (Almsgiving or good deeds), Siyam (Fasting) and Hajj (Pilgrimage).

I like to think of the translation process as taking a poem through a turnstile from the source language and culture into the target language and culture. In that metaphor, Iyad and I are constantly going back and forth through the linguistic and cultural turnstile. Taking the poem through the turnstile involves also taking the poet, and this requires us not only to understand what we have each written, but also to understand each other. For Susan Sontag, literature is like the circulatory system of the world with translation as the plasma, the cells that carry the life-blood. In her 2002 St Jerome Lecture dedicated to the memory of W.G. Sebald, she expressed the view that 'every language is part of Language which is larger than any single language. Every individual literary work is a part of Literature, which is larger than the literature

تمهيد

تيسّا رانسفورد
ترجمة إياد حياتله

إلتقيت بإياد للمرّة الأولى من خلال مشاركته مع "سيرفايفرز برس"، وهي مجموعة أنشأها الشاعر جيري لوس لنشر أعمال الكتّاب الذي عانوا شكلاً من أشكال الأذى النفسي أو الجسدي. إياد فلسطيني من سوريا كان طالباً للجوء في أسكتلندا، وقد تقدّم بطلب للإنضمام إلى "القلم الأسكتلندي" وبعد حيازته العضويّة بدأ المشاركة في النشاطات عام 2003. وقد ساهمتُ أنا وسايمون بيري في إنشاء لجنة جديدة للكتّاب في المنفى بعد أن خلفته في رئاسة القلم الأسكتلندي في نفس العام، وكانت النتيجة المثمرة لذلك سلسلة من ورشات الترجمة والمطبوعات الصغيرة والأمسيات بين كتّاب أسكتلنديين وآخرين مهاجرين من أقطار مختلفة، وقد نُظم كل ذلك وأُدير بشكل رئيسي من قبل الشاعرة إي سي كلارك بالتنسيق مع مجموعة "فنّانون في المنفى، غلاسكو". والتي خلالها ترجم إياد أربعاً من قصائدي إلى العربيّة وأنا ترجمتُ أربعاً من قصائده إلى الإنكليزيّة.

بعد حصول إياد على الجنسيّة البريطانيّة، إعتزمنا سويّة العمل على مشروع تعاوني أكبر لإستكشاف ثقافاتنا الخاصة ومعتقداتنا الدينيّة. وقررنا اتّخاذ عناوين أركان الإسلام الخمسة وكتابة قصائد مستوحاة منها، على أن يترجم كلٌّ منّا قصائد الآخر، منفتحين إلى ما يمكن أن نتعلّمه خلال هذه العمليّة، واضعين نصب أعيننا هدف التعزيز المشترك للتكامل والتفاهم والصداقة. الأركان الخمسة هي: الشهادة، الصلاة، الزكاة، الصيام، والحج.

يعجبني التفكير في أنّ عمليّة الترجمة تشبه إدخال قصيدة خلال الباب الدوار من لغة وثقافة المصدر إلى اللغة والثقافة الهدف. بهذا التشبيه، أنا وإياد نعبر باستمرار الباب الدوّار للغة والثقافة ذهاباً وإياباً. أخذ القصيدة من هذا الباب يتطلّب أخذ الشاعر أيضاً، ممّا يعني أنّه لا يكفي أن نفهم ما نكتبه، بل يجب أن نفهم بعضنا البعض أيضاً. ترى سوزان سونتاغ أنّ الأدب مثل الدورة الدمويّة للعالم والترجمة هي البلازما والخلايا التي تحمل دم الحياة. في محاضرتها في سانت جيروم المخصصة لذكرى و ج سيبالد عام 2002 أكّدت الرأي القائل بأنّ "كل لغة هي جزءٌ من لغة أكبر من أيّ لغة، وأنّ كل عمل

of a single language.' It is in this wide context that the detailed work of translation undertaken by Iyad and me should be understood.

No translation is perfect, in as much as no translation can duplicate the original poem. That is not the aim. The aim is to find an equivalent mode, which will have an equivalent effect on a readership in another language. The territory and the population both change when you are through the turnstile. Therefore the creature you are taking into new territory has to be turned around in order to 'get through' to this new audience. My aim is to make the best possible poem in English, having taken the original poem through the linguistic turnstile. With Arabic it is revealing how similar the structural rhythms are to the English, so that the rhythm can often be carried over without too much difficulty.

The translation process begins with Iyad making his own first translation of each of his poems from Arabic into English. Although I cannot read or speak Arabic, I have learnt Urdu in the past, which has some Arabic roots. We then discuss his translation line by line, word by word, so that I can understand the concept, idiom or picture he has in mind, and I may suggest other possible translations. From that stage, we negotiate towards agreement over the translation. We are happy to leave some phrases that are unusual or sound un-english, if they are right for the poem. Sometimes we re-structure the lay-out of the poem. Iyad's poems are in general more expressive, rhetorical and passionate than the average modern poem in English. I like this and want to allow the lyricism to come through without seeming overdone.

Since the word-play and allusions are sometimes quite dense in my poems, when Iyad is translating them into Arabic there may be a need to explain an allusion or reference, in order for Iyad to find an Arabic expression to relate to the concept or idea in English.

The first poem in the Five Pillars of Islam sequence is 'Testimony', where Iyad describes how the intoning of the *athan*, known to us as 'the call to prayer', at birth, all through life and on the deathbed permeates all Muslim life. (When someone is near to death, a friend or relative is relied upon to 'prompt' or encourage the final recitation.). This poem speaks to the seagulls and doves which perilously visit the high ledges of buildings in Glasgow and seem without 'home'. Iyad asks to be devoured and thus carried as seed in the crops of birds to his homeland where his mother is laying out his poems on the roof in the sun. Iyad's poems are in such ways highly imaginative and full of references to Islamic myth and folklore.

أدبي هو جزءٌ من أدب أكبر من أدب لغةٍ واحدة". وعليه، فالعمل المفصّل للترجمة الذي نقوم به أنا وإياد يجب أن يُفهم في هذا السياق الواسع النطاق.

لا يوجد ترجمةٌ تامّة، كما أنّه لا يمكن لترجمة أن تنسخ القصيدة كصورة طبق الأصل، والهدف ليس هذا، إنّما إيجاد صيغةٍ معادلةٍ يكون لها تأثير مماثل على قرّاء اللغة الأخرى. الأرض والسكان يتغيّران في الباب الدوّار، وهكذا، ينبغي للمخلوق الذي تأخذه إلى أرضٍ جديدة أن يُحوّل ليعبر إلى الجمهور الجديد. هدفي هو جعل القصيدة على أفضل وجهٍ ممكن باللغة الإنكليزية، بعد تمريرها من باب اللغة الدوار، مع الكشف عن مدى تشابه البنى الإيقاعيّة بين العربيّة والإنكليزيّة، ممّا يتيح لهذا الإيقاع الانتقال دون صعوبةٍ كبيرةٍ في كثيرٍ من الأحيان.

تبدأ عمليّة الترجمة عندما يقوم إياد بترجمته الخاصّة الأولى لكل قصيدة من قصائده من العربيّة إلى الإنكليزيّة. ومع أنّي لا أقرأ ولا أتكلّم العربيّة، فقد تعلمت اللغة الأورديّة والتي تمتلك جذوراً عربيّة في الماضي. بعد ذلك نناقش ترجمته كلمة كلمة وسطراً سطراً، حتّى أستطيع أن أفهم الفكرة والعبارة والصورة التي في مخيّلته، وربّما أقترح عليه ترجمة مختلفة ممكنة. ونتفاوض في تلك المرحلة للوصول إلى إتفاقٍ على الترجمة. كما نكون سعيدين بترك بعض العبارات التي تبدو غريبة أو ليست متوائمة مع الإنكليزية إذا كان وجودها في القصيدة مناسباً. كما نقوم أحياناً بإعادة ترتيب نسق القصيدة. وعموماً قصائد إياد أكثر تعبيراً وبلاغةً وعاطفةً من متوسّط القصيدة الإنكليزية المعاصرة. وأنا معجبةٌ بهذا وأريد لغنائيّتها أن تنساب دون أن يبدو أنّها مبالغٌ بها.

ولأنّ اللعب بالكلمات والتلميحات كثيفة جداً أحيانا في قصائدي، فقد يكون هناك حاجة لتوضيح تلميح هنا أو إشارةٍ هناك، كي يتمكن إياد من إيجاد التعبير العربي المناسب لإيصال المفهوم أو الفكرة في اللغة الإنكليزية أثناء الترجمة إلى العربية.

القصيدة الأولى في سلسلة أركان الإسلام هي "الشهادة"، حيث يصف إياد أنّ ترتيل الأذان، والمعروف لدينا بنداء الصلاة، يصاحب المسلم في كل عمره، عند الولادة وطوال الحياة وعلى فراش الموت، (عندما يقوم صديقٌ أو قريب بتلقين أو تشجيع المسلم المقبل على الموت لترتيل شهادته الأخيرة). هذه القصيدة تخاطب النوارس وطيور الحمام التي تبدو بدون وطن وهي تُخاطرُ بزياراتها إلى شرفات الأبنية العالية في غلاسكو. يطلب منها إياد أن تلتهمه وتحمله كالبذور في حوصلاتها إلى وطنه، حيث تنشر والدته قصائده على سطح البيت تحت الشمس. ومن هذا القبيل تبدو قصائد إياد غنيّة بالخيال الواسع وملأى بالإشارات إلى الأساطير الإسلامية والفولكلور.

For another Palestinian poet, Mahmoud Darwish, 'the metaphor of Palestine is stronger than the real Palestine. The metaphor becomes a form of home for the homeless and power for the powerless.' He writes: 'I have built my homeland and found my state in my language.' There's no doubt that this is also the case with Iyad. In translating his work it is important for him not to lose the potency of that metaphorical home, representing the real homeland from which his parents were exiled.

We began by translating each other's poems on Prayer and Fasting, followed by Iyad translating my poems on Almsgiving and Testimony. Iyad's introductory poem 'Fifty' speaks of his birth, and his grandfather singing the call to prayer into his right ear, and of his childhood and family. This is echoed in his poem 'Prayer' where he himself recites into his baby's right ear 'the tuneful *athan*' of the Muslim call to prayer, when the child is born in a Glasgow hospital. He is comforted by the congregation of fellow-worshippers both in Syria and in Glasgow for prayers at the mosque, although in Syria he can identify the place where his father used to stand to pray. Here 'in the mosques of the land of frost', there are people from all over the world, 'like a rug of a thousand colours.'

In his poem 'Hajj'(Pilgrimage), Iyad refers to the rituals required of the pilgrims and to the Qur'anic texts which inspire them, while imagining himself performing them, even as he internalises them. We learn of the story of Hagar and Ishmael from the Qur'an and its variation from that in Genesis. Iyad also alludes to the freedom movements in the Middle East during the Spring of 2011, and in particular to a poem by Abu-al Qasim Alshabi chanted by the crowds in Tunis. In his poem 'Zakat' (Almsgiving), we have the concepts of sharing in suffering, of purification and of taking on the responsibility ourselves to 'weave a sun' in order to give warmth and light to new hopes.

It is apparent that the Five Pillars as interpreted by Muslims are public ritual, although held with inward passion, in a common sense of belonging and being sustained, in comparison with a more personal and isolated Christian version. Similarly, in fasting we may personally give up or forsake something, whereas for the Muslim to fast is to experience physical hunger as a symbol of spiritual hunger for righteousness and justice. This is in fact closer even to our own injunction from Jesus in the Beatitudes: 'Blessed are they which do hunger and thirst after righteousness, for they shall be filled.' (Matthew 5:6)

بالنسبة لشاعر فلسطيني آخر كمحمود درويش، تبدو الإستعارة الفلسطينية أقوى من فلسطين الحقيقية نفسها. حيث تصبح شكلاً من أشكال البيت للمشردين، والقوّة للضعفاء. عندما يكتب: "لقد بنيت وطني ووجدت دولتي في لغتي". وليس هنالك أدنى شك بأنّ هذا هو الحال أيضاً مع إياد. فمن المهم جداً لديه ألاّ يُنتقص من قوّة الوطن المجازي أثناء ترجمة أعماله، لتمثيل الوطن الحقيقي الذي نُفي منه والداه.

بدأنا بترجمة قصائد بعضنا بقصيدتي الصلاة والصوم، تلا ذلك ترجمة إياد قصيدتي عن الزكاة والشهادة، أمّا قصيدة إياد الإستهلالية "خمسون" فهي تتحدث عن مولده، وترتيل جدّه الأذان في أذنه اليمنى، وطفولته وعائلته. وقد تردد صدى ذلك في قصيدته عن الصلاة، حيث أنشد هو نفسه ذلك الأذان الرخيم في أذن طفله الذي ولد في مشفى غلاسكو. أيضاً يذكر كيف كان يشعر بالتشجيع والراحة بين حشود المصلّين في مساجد سوريا وغلاسكو، بالإضافة إلى أنّه استطاع تمييز الركن الذي تعوّد والده أن يصلّي فيه. وهنا "في مساجد أرض الصقيع" وجد أناساً من جميع أنحاء العالم، "كسجّادة من ألف لون".

في قصيدته "الحج" يشير إياد إلى الشعائر الواجبة على الحجّاج وإلى النصوص القرآنيّة التي توحي بذلك، متخيّلاً نفسه أنّه يقوم بتأديتها بصفته الذاتيّة. هنا نتعلّم قصة هاجر وإسماعيل من القرآن وإختلافها عمّا نعرفه في سفر التكوين. يشير إياد أيضاً إلى حركات التحرر في الشرق الأوسط خلال ربيع عام 2011, وعلى وجه الخصوص إلى قصيدة أبي القاسم الشابّي التي أنشدت من قبل الحشود في تونس. في قصيدته "الزكاة", تظهر لدينا مفاهيم المشاركة في المعاناة والتطهير وأخذ المسؤوليّة على عاتقنا لكي "ننسج الشمس" بغرض منح الدفء والضوء للآمال الجديدة.

من الواضح أنّ أركان الإسلام الخمسة هي طقوس عامّة كما فسّرها المسلمون، ومع أنّها متوافقة مع العاطفة الباطنيّة، بالإحساس المشترك بالإنتماء والدعم المستمر، مقارنةً مع نسخة مسيحيّة معزولة وأكثر خصوصيّة. بالمثل، قد نتخلّى عن شيء ما بشكل شخصي في الصيام، في حين أنّه يعني للمسلم تجربة الجوع المادي باعتباره رمزاً للجوع الروحي للبرّ والعدل. وهذا في الواقع أقرب إلى وصيّتنا الواردة في تطويبات المسيح: "طوبى للذين يجوعون ويعطشون لأجل البرّ، لأنّهم سيشبعون". (متّى 5:6).

Allusions and references are part of my emotional and mental structure and are not esoteric for my generation, but may be so for the younger generations in Britain today, whether they are church attenders or no. When I refer to the 'dayspring from on high' in 'Morning Prayer' and the 'daystar in my heart' I am quoting from 1 Peter:19 — 'until the daystar arise in your hearts' and Zacharias' hymn of praise on the birth of John the Baptist in Luke 1:78 –'the dayspring from on high hath visited us'. In 'Evening Prayer', I open with the familiar child's evening hymn 'Now the Day is Over' and in my poem 'Prayer' I allude to Milton's poem 'On his blindness' with the much-loved line: 'they also serve who only stand and wait'. In my poem on Pilgrimage I evoke images from Chaucer's *The Canterbury Tales* and from Bunyan's *Pilgrim's Progress*. I quote from Thoreau about the cost of a thing being the amount of 'life' we give to it in my poem on Almsgiving and echo the anchoress Julian of Norwich in 'Midmorning prayer': 'all manner of thing being well'.

Thus literature and the spiritual are integrated in our culture. Scottish academic, Cairns Craig, has suggested that we all live in 'sedimented layers of culture'. We know, nowadays, that we live in one world wherever we are, and that translation is a door that opens doors into this unity, rich with variety.

Tessa Ransford

التلميحات والإشارات هي جزءٌ من بنائي الذهني والعاطفي وهي ليست مقصورة على جيلي، ولكن قد تكون كذلك أيضاً بالنسبة للأجيال الشابة في بريطانيا اليوم، سواء كانوا من المترددين للكنيسة أم لا. عندما أشير إلى 'انبلاج الفجر من الأعالي' في قصيدتي 'صلاة الصبح' و إلى 'الشمس في قلبي' فأنا أقتبس من (إنجيل بطرس 1:19): 'حتّى تشرق الشمس في قلوبكم' وترتيل زكريّا في الثناء على ولادة يوحنّا المعمدان في (إنجيل لوقا 1:78): 'إنبلاج الفجر الذي زارنا من الأعالي'. في 'صلاة المساء': أبدأ بترنيمة الطفل المسائيّة المعروفة 'إنتهى اليوم الآن' وفي قصيدتي 'صلاة' أشير إلى قصيدة "ميلتون" 'في عماه' مع البيت المحبوب جداً: 'إنّهم أيضاً يخدمون الذي يقف وينتظر فقط'. في قصيدتي عن الحج أستحضر صوراً من (حكايات كانتربري، لتشوسر) ومن (تقدّم الحجّاج، لبنيان). وأقتبس عن (ثورو) أنّ كلفة الشيء تكون بكميّة 'الحياة' التي نمنحه لها، وذلك في قصيدتي عن الزكاة، أمّا في قصيدتي 'صلاة الضحى' فأرددّ صدى (جوليان راهبة نورويتش): 'كل شيء على طريق الرفاه'.

وهكذا يتكامل الأدب والروحانيّة في ثقافتينا. وقد أفاد الأكاديمي الأسكتلندي كيرنز كريغ بأنّنا جميعاً نعيش في 'الطبقات الرسوبيّة للثقافة'. وهذه الأيّام، نحن نعلم أنّنا نعيش في عالم واحد أينما كنّا، والترجمة هي الباب الذي يفتح أبوابه على الوحدة الغنيّة بتنوّعها.

Introduction

WHEN TESSA FIRST suggested this idea to me, I was anxious about it as much as I liked it. Any discussion of Islam to a non-Muslim audience involves many sensitive issues – it may be seen as an invitation to convert or as implying that one religion is preferable to another. I was also aware of those Muslims who might consider my giving my name to poems inspired by the Pillars of Islam as an insult to the holiness of this religion.

Eventually, my enthusiasm for this project overcame my worries as I realised the importance of delivering a message that Islam is not a religion of rituals and rites only, but a method for living the entire life; and that human experience has an important role in establishing and strengthening good relations among Muslims themselves, and between Muslims and non-Muslim societies. I also wanted to provide for the western reader an image of Islam that differs from the one presented by the media.

This series of poems is presented by a Muslim Arabic poet, who has suffered much from being an exile both from his ancestral hometown, which he has never seen, and now from his second place of refuge. They explore the effect of this experience of practising his religion in these different places of exile.

It is important to point out that the poem 'Fifty' was not a part of this project, but Tessa and I decided to include it as it makes a good introduction to the presence of religion in the outward and inward aspects of a Muslim's life from the very moment of birth. In addition, this poem documents the first fifty years of my journey in this life. Another matter to clarify, is that these poems were not inspired one from the other, nor were they written as responses to each other, they were written completely separately and individually. Tessa and I did not read each other's poems until there were finalised; therefore any similarity in ideas or any suggested telepathy is accidental. Nevertheless it is not mere coincidence, and gives assurance of our similar understanding for the role of religion in the life of individuals and society.

تمهيد

إياد حياتله

عندما طرحت تيسّا الفكرة عليّ، تخوّفتُ منها بالقدر الذي رحّبتُ بها، وجاء تخوّفي لأنّ الحديث عن الإسلام لجمهور غير مسلم يحمل في طيّاته حساسيات كثيرة، ليس أقلّها الإعتقاد بأنّها محاولة للدعوة وتفضيل دينٍ على آخر، ومن جهةٍ أخرى كان الخوف من تفسير البعض لإضفاء طابع التجربة الشخصية إلى قصائد تتحدث عن أركان الإسلام، أنّه محاولةٌ للنيل من قداسة هذا الدين.

ولكنّ حماسي للمشروع تغلّب على قلقي لأنني رأيت من الأهميّة بمكان إيصال رسالة أنّ الإسلام ليس دين طقوس وشعائر فقط بل هو منهاج حياة، وللحس الإنساني دورٌ كبيرٌ إنتشاره، وتمتين أواصر العلاقة الطيبة بين منتسبيه من جهة، وبينهم وبين المجتمعات الأخرى من جهة ثانية، أيضاً أردت أن أقدّم للقارئ الغربي صورة مختلفة عما تمطره بها وسائل الإعلام عن الإسلام والمسلمين، من شاعر عربي مسلم عانى الأمرّين بسبب لجوءه عن بلده الذي لم يره أصلاً، وأيضاً بسبب لجوئه من منفاه الأول إلى منفىً آخر، ومدى انعكاس هذه التجربة على تفاصيل ممارسته لدينه في منافيه المتعددة.

ولا بدّ من التنويه في البداية أنّ قصيدة "خمسون" ليست جزءًا من المشروع، ولكن أنا وتيسّا ارتأينا ضمّها لهذه المجموعة لأنّها تشكّل مدخلا جيّدا للحديث عن وجود الدين في ظاهر وباطن حياة المسلم منذ لحظة ولادته، بالإضافة لكون هذه القصيدة توثّق لرحلتي لخمسين عاماً في هذه الحياة بقالب شعري، أيضاً نريد أن نوضّح أنّ هذه القصائد لم تُكتب من وحي بعضها البعض أو كردود على بعضها البعض، بل كُتبت كلٌّ على حده وبشكل منفصل، وأنا وتيسّا لم نطّلع على قصائد الآخر إلاّ بعد انتهائها، وكل توارد للخواطر أو تشابه في الأفكار لم يأتِ عن تخطيطٍ مسبق، وأيضاً ليس هو محض صدفةٍ خالصة، بل هو تأكيدٌ على تشابه فهمنا لدور الدين في حياة الإنسان والمجتمع.

I did not intend to impose rhymes on the Arabic translation of Tessa's poems, yet I have done my best to preserve each poetic image while translating the meaning. This task may look easy at first glance but certainly it is not; for Tessa, being unable to read her poems in Arabic, has placed on me a greater responsibility to produce a trustworthy script that matches the original one and carries a similar value of beauty and creativity.

Tessa's poem 'Testimony' opens with a list of words and expressions which are close in sound and connected in sense to describe her understanding of faith. While she wrote a general poem about prayer that included a quotation from the English poet Milton, she also wrote a sequence of poems about prayer at different times of the day that clearly corresponds to the changing phases of life. In her poem 'Almsgiving', which starts with a quotation from the American writer and poet Henry David Thoreau, she expresses a humane concept of extreme selflessness, self-denial and sharing of everything in this life. In her poem 'Fasting', she suggests that trying to stop from the daily needs of work and study, is much more difficult than ceasing to eat for a period. She starts her poem about pilgrimage with imaginary pictures of Chaucer's *Canterbury Tales*, then moves to some kind of conversation between characters in Bunyan's *Pilgrim's Progress* in such a way that shows her belief that life is a continual pilgrimage.

Athan is mentioned in several places through my poems. It is the Islamic call for prayer and the first thing a newborn Muslim hears when a parent says the *athan* in the child's right ear. This is an intensely personal moment and makes a perfect setting for a memory-image in the poem, especially when this happens in exile. That is why it is repeated more than once. In my poem 'Testimony', I travel with poetry from my place of birth to my place of residence and back to the place where I wish to die with the speed of anxious imagination, and nothing calms my anxiety except the presence of the testimony at the beginning and the end of the poem, which represents the beginning and the end of the life itself. That serenity is revealed again in my poem 'Prayer'; serenity that comes to the soul when we pray for ourselves or for others; the serenity of praying for mercy for my father who died as a stranger away from his hometown; the serenity of praying with my Muslim brothers, gathered from all over the world, in a country that does not speak the language of their prayer.

في ترجمتي لقصائد تيسًا فإنّي لم أعمد إلى فرض قوافٍ على النص العربي، ولكن حـاولـت جهـدي المزواجة بين ترجمة المفردة ونقل الصورة الشعرية، وهي مهمّة ربّما تبدو سهلة في ظاهرها، ولكنّها ليست كذلك تماماً، حيث عدم معرفة تيسًا باللغة العربية يجعلها عاجزة عـن متابعـة نصّـها باللغـة الجديدة، وهذا ما حمّلني مسؤولية أكبر لإنتاج نصٍّ أمينٍ للنص الأصلي ويحمل نفس القيمة الإبداعيـة والجمالية.

في قصيدتها "الشهادة" استخدمت الشاعرة الكلمات والتعابير المتداخلة متشابهة اللفظ مختلفـة طريقـة الكتابة بشكل موفق، في محاولة منها لإعطاء مفهوم أوسع لنظرتها للعقيدة، بينما كتبت الشاعرة قصيدة عامة عن الصلاة ضمّنتها اقتباسا للشاعر الإنكليزي "ميلتون نيو"، أيضاً كتبت سلسلة قصـائد عـن الصلاة في أوقات اليوم المختلفة في إشارة واضحة إلى مراحل التحوّل في عمر الإنسـان، أمّـا فـي قصيدتها عن الزكاة التي بدأتها باقتباس شهير عن الشاعر الأمريكي "هنري ديفيد ثورو"، فقد عبّـرت الشاعرة عن مفهوم إنساني غايةً في التفاني والإيثار والتشاركيّة في كلّ شيءٍ في هـذه الحيـاة، وفـي قصيدتها عن الصيّام أكّدت الشاعرة أنّ التوقف عن العمل وعن البحث والمعرفة والتطوّر هو أصـعب بمراحل من التوقف عن الطعام لفترة معيّنة، بينما افتتحت قصيدتها عن الحج بصورٍ متخيّلـة عـن "حكايات كانتربري، لجيفري تشوسر" منتقلة بعد ذلك إلى إدخال حوارات بعض شخصيّات "تقدّم الحج، لجون بنيان" بما يخدم نظرتها في أنّ الحياة رحلةُ حجٍّ دائمة ومتواصلة في آن واحد.

في غير موضع من قصائدي يأتي ذكر "الأذان" وهو نداء الصلاة وهو أوّل ما يجب أن يسمعه المولود المسلم، بأن يقوم والده أو جدّه أو أيّ رجل من المتواجدين بتلقين الطفل هذا الأذان في أذنـه اليمنـى، وهي لحظة شديدة الإنسانيّة والوجد مُرتكزا جيّدا لتأسيس ذاكرة للقصيـدة وخصوصـا عنـدما يحصل هذا في الغربة، وهذا ما يفسّر تكرارها لديّ في أكثر من واحدة، في قصيدتي "شهادة" أسافر مع الشعر بين مكان ولادتي ومكان إقامتي والمكان المرتجى لموتي بسرعة الخيال القلق، ولا يسكّـن هـذا القلق إلى وجود التشّهد في بداية ونهاية القصيدة، بداية ونهاية الحياة، بينما في قصيدتي "صـلاة" تبـدو السكينة التي تهبط على الإنسان وهو يصلّي لأجله ولأجل الآخرين ملازمة للقصيدة، سـكينة الـدعاء بالرحمة لوالدي الذي مات غريباً عن وطنه، وسكينةُ الصّلاة مع أخوةٍ لم تلدهم والدتي تجمّعوا من كـل حدبٍ وصوبٍ في بلادٍ لا تتحدّث لغة صلاتهم.

In my poem 'Almsgiving' I show my understanding of 'Zakat'. As a general concept it is not only the obligation to alms in Islam, that is to give 2.5 per cent of one's wealth every year for the poor, but I extend it to include the importance of sharing the happiness and sadness of life before it is too late, inspired by the saying of the prophet Mohammad, peace be upon him: 'Your smile to the face of your brother is an alms'. The meaning of hunger in the poem 'Fasting' varies between its real and metaphorical meanings, the hunger for food and the longing for the lover or the homeland, where fasting from food seems much easier. In this poem I also mention the 'powerful night', which is an odd-numbered night at the end of Ramadan month, when Muslims believe that the doors of the heavens are opened wide and the mighty Allah responds to their prayers.

In my last poem, 'Hajj', I try to link the description of steps and rituals of pilgrimage (which I have yet to perform myself), with the story of building the Ka'ba, interweaving it with verses from the Holy Qur'an where it is mentioned, and acknowledging that this pilgrimage will not be complete without the freedom of Jerusalem and Al-Aqsa Mosque, which has a very high status for Muslims. The poet here is dreaming, and may be wishing to achieve this liberation in the light of the Arab Spring and the demand of all Arabic people for freedom, inspired by the famous line of poetry by the Tunisian poet Abu-al Qasim Alshabi: 'When people demand real life, fate must respond accordingly.'

Iyad Hayatleh
Translated with Osama Hayatleh

في قصيدتي "زكاة" يبدو واضحاً أنّني أنظر للزكاة في معناها الأشمل، وهي التي لا تقتصر فقط على الزكاة المفروضة على المال في الإسلام، بأن توزّع ما يعادل 2.5% من ثروتك على الفقراء في كل عام، بل تتعدّى ذلك إلى مشاركة الغير أفراح وأتراح الحياة قبل فوات الأوان، مستوحياً حديث الرسول صلّى الله عليه وسلّم: "تبسّمك في وجه أخيك صدقة"، في قصيدة "صيام" يتراوح عندي الجوع بين معناه الحقيقي والمجازي، الجوع للطعام، والشوق للحبيب أو للوطن، حيث يبدو الصيام عن الطعام أسهل كثيرا، أيضاً يرد ذكر "ليلة القدر"، وهي ليلة تكون في إحدى الليالي المفردة في العشر الأواخر من رمضان، حيث يعتقد المسلمون أنّ أبواب السماء تكون مفتوحة خلالها، وأنّ الله يستجيب لدعواتهم.

في قصيدتي الأخيرة "الحج" حاولتُ المزاوجة بين وصف شعائر وخطوات الحج الذي لم أؤدّه بعد، وبين قصّة بناء "الكعبة" كما وردت في القرآن الكريم، مستخدما تناصّا مع آياته الكريمه، معتبراً أن الحج لا يكتمل إلاّ بتحرير القدس والمسجد الأقصى ذو المكانة الرفيعة عند المسلمين، حالماً وممنّياً النفس بتحقيق ذلك في ضوء الربيع العربي ومطلب الشعب العربي بالتحرر مستوحياً بيت الشعر الشهير للشاعر التونسي "أبو القاسم الشابي":

إذا الشعبّ يوماً أراد الحياة   فلا بدّ أن يستجيب القدَرْ

Fifty

by Iyad Hayatleh
translated with Tessa Ransford

There – far away
where the sky, just a bow's length from a sigh,
overshadows the roofs of the houses
born out of tents
as it dries the tears of old women
who weep for the warmth of homes they left –
which remain on their eyelashes
wherever they dwell
wherever they go

There – far away
fifty years ago
I shook hands with the bustle of life for the first time
drew in the breath of the midwife
of that tin-housed neighbourhood

held upside down
as my little body sensed the air of the camp
beneath me the roof of the barracks
then, rocked to her heart,
I clasped my angel who shared her soul with me;
I fed at her breast on poetry
and the catastrophe of my people

خمسونُ

بعيداً هنالكَ
حيثُ السّماءُ على قابِ آهٍ
تُظِلُّ سَقفَ البيوتِ التي خَلّفتها الخِيامُ
تُجَفّفُ دَمعَ العواجيزِ يبكونَ دفءَ البيوتِ التي خَلّفوها
وَظَلّت بأهدابِهمْ أينَ حلّوا وقاموا

بَعيداً هنالكَ – مِن قبلِ خمسينَ –
صافَحتُ للمرّةِ البِكر صَخبَ الحياةِ
تَنَفّستُ للمرّة البِكرِ زفراتِ دايَةِ حيّ الصّفيحِ
رَأيتُ على الأرضِ سَقفَ البَرَكْسِ
ولامسَ جسمي الضّئيلُ هواءَ المخيّمِ
عانقتُ قلبي،
مَلاكي التي روحَها قاسمتني
قصيدَ الحياةِ،
وَنكبةَ أهلي حليباً تقطّرَ من صدرها أرضعتنيَّ

There –
in my right ear
rang for the first time the tuneful *athan*
I heard his sympathetic voice
when he, who seeing nothing,
asked for me, saying
I want to see him
when birds brought him tidings of my festive arrival
and doves sang in my welcome

There – far away
fifty years ago
sixty or more
when my playful father was still a lad
and I but a seed in his loins
it was even then that I took the first steps of my exodus
on that woeful path
I held in my patience
the prickly pear of the orchards
and fed on its spines in the lean years;
I allowed hope to seep through my bones
covered myself with nostalgia
yet on dark nights nothing covered me
except the mighty skies

winds blow me in every direction:
the bitter waiting
plants passion and tenderness in my heart
north and east, south and west
north to the west, north to north
to remote coasts where no further north exists

هُنالكَ،

رنّ بأذني اليمينِ

وللمرّةِ البِكرِ أيضاً رخيمُ الأذانِ

وصوتُ الذي لا يراني

– بكلِّ الحنانِ – أتاني

أيا مرحباً،

أعطُونيهِ أراهُ

فقدْ بَشّرتني بِعُرسِ القُدومِ الطّيورُ وغنّى الحمامُ

بَعيداً هنالكَ مِن قبلِ خمسينَ

مِنْ قبلِ بِضعٍ وستّينَ – في صُلْبِ ذاكَ الشّقيِّ –

افْتَتحتُ بِدربِ المواجعِ سِفرَ المنافي

حَملتُ على حَرفِ قلبيَ صَبرَ الحواكيرِ

أقتاتُ أشواكَهُ في سِنيِّ العِجافِ

أُمَنّي العِظامَ بِسودِ الليالي الحنينَ لِحافاً

ولا شيءَ إلاّ بُروجُ السّماءِ لِحافي

تُبعثِرني الرّيحُ أينَ استدارتْ

ويزرعُ مُرُّ انتظاري جَوىً في شِغافي

شَمالاً فشرقاً

جَنوباً فغرباً

شَمالاً فغرباً، شَمالاً شَمالاً إلى نائياتِ الضّقافِ

وحيثُ لم يبقَ بعدَ الشّمالِ شمالٌ يُرامُ

and I
neither returned whence I came
nor did my soul touch the ground
where my grandma walked barefooted;
where my heart lighted its smouldering lanterns
where my forefathers' bones dissolved in that soil
finding rest in its depths

As though, O life,
you began yesterday
as though, O yesterday,
for fifty years, O yesterday,
you have been sleeping in my eyes

I see myself
crawl, pull out straws from the matting,
ride on the back of my blind grandpa like a brave knight,
sleep on my grandma's lap
on the sheepskin made from the Eid lamb
infiltrating her dream to return;
as though, O life,
you began yesterday
it is as if those who mounted the steeds of death
ages ago
have resided always in my heart

When I turn with some greeting at night
they respond at once
saying, be well
as their faces shine with smiles;
just before dawn

وما عُدتُ يوماً لحيثُ ابْتدأتُ
وَلا مَسَّتِ الرّوحُ أرضاً مَشَتْ جَدّتي فَوقها حافِيَهْ
وَأَوقَدَ فيها فُؤادي قَناديلَهُ الغافِيَهْ
وَذابَتْ عِظامُ جُدودي بِتُربَتِها الصّافِيَهْ
وَطابَ لَهُم في التّجاويفِ مِنها المَقامُ

كَأَنَّكَ يا عُمرُ أمسِ ابْتَدأتَ
كَأَنَّكَ يا أمسُ
– مِن قبلِ خَمسينَ – في طرفِ عيني تَنامُ

أرانيَ أحبو وأنتفُ قشَّ الحصيرِ
على ظهرِ جدّي الكفيفِ،
أنا فارسُ العادياتِ الهُمامُ
وفي حُضنِ سِتّي عَلى جاعدِ العيدِ
مُسترِقاً حُلمَها بالرّجوعِ أنامُ

كَأَنَّكَ يا عُمرُ أمسِ ابْتَدأتَ
كَأَنَّ الذينَ امْتَطوا مَوتهمْ مُنذُ دَهرٍ
عَلى خافِقي مُنذُ دَهرٍ أقاموا
إذا ما الْتَفتُّ بِبعضِ سلامٍ بليلٍ
يُرَدُّ على الفورِ مِنهم بِأحسنَ مِنهُ السّلامُ
يَقولونَ أهلا
ويُشرقُ فوقَ الوجوهِ قُبَيلَ انْبِلاجِ الصّباحِ ابْتِسامُ

IYAD HAYATLEH AND TESSA RANSFORD

they are far however near I come
they are near however far I go;
they are enshrined in my being

Near or far, far is always

There – far away
where the sky's just a bow's length from a sigh
fifty years ago
those were the throes of the beginning

Here – far away
where the sky's just a bow's length from a tomb and weeping
fifty years later
I trust it is not the final agony that I face
and that darkness does not spread

بعيدونَ مهما اقتربتُ
قريبونَ مهما ابتعدتُ
فُؤادي لَهمْ جَنّةٌ ومقامُ

بَعيداً هُنالكَ حيثُ السّماءُ على قابِ آهٍ ولَوعَهْ
بَعيداً هنالكَ مِن قبلِ خمسينَ كانَ مَخاضُ البِدايَه

بَعيداً هُنا حَيثُ تَجثو السّماءُ على قابِ قبرٍ وَدَمعهْ
بَعيداً هُنا بعدَ خمسينَ آمَلُ ألاّ يُخطُّ نِزاعُ النِهايَه
وألاّ يعمَّ الظلامُ.

The Five Pillars of Islam

أركان الإسلام الخمسة

Shahada (Testimony)

by Iyad Hayatleh
translated with Tessa Ransford

Laughter and tears come together
when one soul makes path for another
and, with the serene voice of *athan*
Allah is Great
Allah is Great
our Muslim birthright is naturally bestowed.

We testify there is none but *Allah*
whom we worship on this earth.
We pray for Mohammed
the latest prophet and messenger.
Here is the source of our belief
where the first page of life is opened.

Life goes by in the blink of an eye,
each chapter written by our ambition.
We leave the mire of the camp,
embrace a continuing diaspora.
We traverse countries, deserts, moors and glens
to reach a riverbank
where seagulls overshadow us.

شهادة

إياد حياتله

إذا ما تمازجَ ضحكٌ بِدمعٍ
وأفسَحتِ الرّوحُ للرّوحِ درباً لكي تَتجدّدْ
فإنّا على شجْوِ صوتِ المؤذّنِ
- اللهُ أكبرُ، اللهُ أكبرُ -
والفِطرةِ الحقِّ - نُولَدْ
فَنشهَدْ
بألاّ إلهَ سِواهُ لِيُعبَدْ
نُصلّي على خاتَمِ الرُسلِ والأنبياءِ مُحمّدْ
هُنا يَبدأُ الإعتقادُ
ويُرسمُ في صَفحةِ المرءِ مَشهدْ

كمَا طَرفةُ العينِ تَمضي الحياةُ
نَخوضُ تَفاصيلها، تَدْفعُنا الأمنياتُ
نُغادرُ طينَ المخيّمِ يَسكنُ فينا الشّتاتُ
نَجوبُ البلادَ صَحارىً، مُروجاً
جِبالاً، وهاداً
ونُفضي لِنهرٍ على ضِفّتيهِ تُظلّـلُنا النَورَساتُ

O you seagulls and doves,
are you strangers like me?
I believe you are
for you are rootless and
there is no home for you on window ledges.

Come, I provide a love-camp for you.
Seek asylum in my heart
    I, the diehard refugee –
Life still beats strongly within me.

ألا يَتُها النورساتُ ..
الحماماتُ ..
غريباتُ أنتنّ مثلِيَ؟
أم لا؟

.. كأنّي بِكنَّ،
فلا وطنٌ في النوافذِ ..
لا أمّهاتُ

.. تَعالَيْنَ ..
صَدري مخيّمُ عَشقٍ
إليهِ التجِأْنَ

.. تَجِدْنَ بقلبي
- أنا اللاجئُ المرُّ -
تَحيا الحياةُ

Come, I am devoured by you
so I may travel as you fly
to scatter me like seed on a rooftop
where my mother lays out my poems in the sun
with tears and songs.

There, decades ago I recited the testimony
and there I wish to be buried –
and I wish that when I am dying
there remains one who will prompt me
in that recital.

تَعالَين
كَيما أوزّعَ بعضي عَلَيْكنَّ
علَّي أسافرُ فيكنَّ
تحملُني الحَوْصلاتُ

وَتَنْعَفُ روحي بِذاراً
على سطحِ بيتٍ
تُشَـــمِّـــسُ أمّي عليهِ
مناديلَ شِعري
بِدمعٍ تُزَنّرُهُ الأغنياتُ

هُناكَ تَلَوْتُ الشّهادةَ قبلَ عُقودٍ
وَكم ذا مُنايَ هُنالكَ أُلْحَدْ
على فرشةِ الموتِ
يَهمِسُ بي مِنْ تَبقّى
تَشَهّدْ ..
تَشَهّدْ ..
تَشَهّدْ ...

Testimony

by Tessa Ransford

Blessing
Bliss
Beauty
Beatitude
Belief
Being
Becoming

Illumination
if even a speck on a manuscript
will hold the hope-line, the tenet

Forgiveness
for those who hurt us
or manipulate us
or put obstacles in our way

شهادة

تيسّا رانسفورد
ترجمة إياد حياتله

بَركةٌ
نَعيمٌ
جمالٌ
تطويبٌ
إيمانٌ
كينونةٌ
تَحوّلٌ

تنويرٌ روحيٌّ
حتّى ولو لبقعةٍ صغيرةٍ جدّاً من مخطوطة
سوفَ تدعمُ التمسّكَ بشعاعِ الأملْ

مغفرةٌ
للذينَ يُؤذوننا
أو يتلاعبونَ بنا
أو يضعونَ العقبات في طريقنا

They are not the ones
we have hurt

Undeceived by glib offers or predictions

Daring to be serious
Fearing the worst
Facing it

Coherence
Co-inherence
Consistency
Carefulness

Children
Climate

Under-standing
Astounding
Withstanding

وَنحن الذينَ لم نُؤذِهم من قبل
ولَم نخدعهم بالنبوءة العفويّة

الجرأةُ لنكونَ جادّين
وخائفينَ من الأسوء
مُجابهينَ له
التلاحُم
التّضمُّن
الإصرار
الدّقة
الأطفال
المناخْ

الوقوف تحت
الإدهاش
الْجَلَدْ

Salah (Prayer)

by Iyad Hayatleh
translated with Tessa Ransford

My God
Lord of a heaven far away from me *there*
near to me *here*
I pray to you *there*, pray to you *here*.
Five decades ago *there*
it was tuneful *athan* rang in my right ear
and eight years ago *here*
I chanted the same *athan*
in my new-born baby's right ear
and showered his cheeks with tears –
one stranger *here* comforts another.
Mother watches behind a curtain of tears and feels pity for us *here*
and an astonished midwife with an open mouth gasps:
What on earth are they doing here?
What is he mumbling in the baby's ear?
dawn, noon, afternoon
sunset and night
each time I pray to the Lord who granted us love, grace and blessing
and poured the light and sap of life into our bodies.

صلاة

إياد حياتله

إلهيَ
ربُّ السّماءِ البعيدةِ عنّي هناكَ
القريبةِ منّي هُنا
إليكَ أصلّي هُناكَ، إليكَ أصلّي هُنا
هُنالكَ مِن قبلِ خمسِ عقودٍ سَمعتُ رخيمَ الأذانِ بأذني اليمين
وقبلَ ثمانٍ شدوتُ بعذبِ الأذانِ بأذنِ وليدي الشّمالِ هُنا
وأغدقتُ دَمعاً على وجنتيه، غريبٌ يُواسي غريباً هُنا
وأمٌّ تُراقبُ خلف ستارِ الدموعِ وتأسو عَلينا هُنا
وقَابلةٌ تفتحُ الثغرَ مشدوهةً: ما الذي يفعلونَ هُنا؟
وَماذا يُتمتمُ ذلكَ في أذنِ هذا؟

نِداءُ الصلاةِ
صَباحاً وظهراً وعصراً
غُروباً عِشاءً،
وفي كلِّ وقتٍ أُصلّي لِربِّ لَنا الخيرَ حُبّاً، عطاءً وهَبْ
وَفي نُسغِنا النّورَ والمعجزاتِ، حياةً سكبْ

IYAD HAYATLEH AND TESSA RANSFORD

I pray for tranquillity to overwhelm my soul
for the right guidance to flow over all the people in the world.
I pray for mercy to fill my heart
for happiness to rise from my eyes.

There
I returned to the neighbourhood mosque
and recognised some faces that bid farewell to me years ago
and my father's wasn't amongst them;
but a corner where he used to pray, perfumed with his breath,
invited me.
I knelt down low and repeatedly pressed my forehead
on what fell from his spirit there
and offered him my tears
and recited the opening verse of the Holy Qur'an by his grave
for a long time.
I cried for him and also wept for my mourning soul.

Here
in the mosques of the land of frost
I met people who came from all over the world.
Like a rug of a thousand colours
we've been unfolded behind the Imam,
a flower from each garden, each has their own tongue
but there is only one language for prayer.
Glorify, saying *God is great*
for the nation praying to the Lord
who sat on the throne of heaven *there*
and who sits on the throne of heaven *here*.

أصلّي، لتَغشى السَّكينةُ روحي
لهديٍ يفيضُ على العالمين بكلِّ الدُّنا
أصلّي، لِيَملأَ قلبي الوِدادُ
وَ يُشرقُ من مقلتيَّ الهَنا.

هُنالكِ في جامعِ الحيِّ أبصرتُ بعضَ الوجوهِ التي ودّعتني قبيلَ سنينِ
وَما كان وجهُ أبي بينهمْ، ولكنَّ ركناً تَعوَّدَ أنفاسَهُ العاطِراتِ دعاني
سَجَدتُ، ومَرَّغتُ وجهاً عَلى ما تَساقطَ مِنْ روحِهِ في المكانِ
وأهدَيتُهُ دَمعتينِ
ورَتَّلتُ دَهراً عَلى قبرِهِ الفاتحهْ،
بَكيتُ عليهِ وأيضاً بكيتُ عُلى روحيَ النّائحهْ.

هُنا
في مساجدِ أرضِ الصَّقيعِ التقيتُ أناساً أتوا مِن جميعِ الجهاتِ
أشقّاءُ ما أنجبَتهمْ ليَ الوالدهْ
كَسجّادةٍ لَونُها ألفُ لونٍ، بِها مِن كلِّ حقلٍ ورودٌ مُدِدْنا وَراءَ الإمامِ

لِكُلٍّ لسانٌ، وصوتُ الصَّلاةِ لَهُ لُغةٌ واحدهْ
فكبِّرْ وَهلِّلْ على أمّةٍ ساجدهْ
لِرَبٍّ تربّعَ عرشَ السّماءِ هُناكَ
وأيضاً تربّعَ عرشَ السّماءِ هُنا.

Prayer-sequence

by Tessa Ransford

I have prayed in panic to the gods of chance
let it not happen
in pain to the angels of healing
let it get better and prayed
to the everlasting wings
for those I love to be safe, well, happy

Everyday I've prayed on waking and sleeping
for support from the powers of goodwill and
to the holy spirit of wisdom
by way of calming myself before an ordeal

But none of this is praying

To pray is to offer ourselves
to accept, be open, listen,
or to be the one who must lose or fail
or wait

سلسلة الصلاة

تيسّا رانسفورد
ترجمة إياد حياتله

صلّيتُ بهلعٍ لآلهة الحظ
مُتمنيّة ألا يحدث
بألمٍ لملائكة الشفاء
متمنيّة أن يتحسّن
وصلّيتُ للأجنحة الخالدة
لأجل أن يكون الذين أحبّهم آمنين، طيّبين، وسُعداء

في كلّ يومٍ صلّيتُ في الصحو والنوم
لأستمدّ الدعم من قوّة الإرادة الطيبّة
لِروحِ الحكمة المقدّسة
كطريقة لتهدئة نفسي قبل المحنة

لكن، ليس كلّ ما سبق صلاة
الصلاةُ أن نَهَبَ أنفسَنا
أن نتقبّلَ، نستمعَ، ونكونَ مُنفتحين
أو نكونَ مستعدّينَ للخسارةِ، أو الفشل والإنتظار

To pray is to let ourselves
be drudges, workhorses,
between the shafts when we could
be winning the steeplechase.

To pray, as blind Milton knew,
is not even to want
circumstances to change
but to believe they will

Morning Prayer

Let me wake to light
to the daystar in my heart
to the sun in my soul
however dark the day
and overcast with pain
with loneliness with grief
with knowledge that hopes
must be for others not myself,
others whom I live or linger for
that they may welcome daily
the dayspring from on high

الصلاةُ هي أن نكونَ مِن الكادحين
أحصنة عملٍ بينَ العمدان
حتّى وإن كنّا نستطيعُ تجاوز حواجز القفز

الصلاةُ أن نكونَ مثل ميلتون نيو الأعمى
ألاّ نكتفي بأنّنا نريد للظروف أن تتغيّر
بل نُؤمن أنّها سوف تتغيّرُ فعلا.

صلاة الصبح

تُوقظني للضوء
للشمسِ في قلبي
للشمس في روحي
مهما كانَ النهارُ معتماً
ومدثّرا بالألم

مع الوحدة والأسى
وبالمعرفةِ الآملة
ليس لي، بل للأجيال الشابة
الذينَ أعيشُ وأبقى لأجلهم
ليستقبلوا انبلاج الصبحِ من الأعالي
كلَّ يوم.

Midmorning Prayer

Let me look forward to what may be
not in my plan not in my wish
but whatever it is
for me
and therefore right, alright
all manner of thing being well

Midday prayer

See Apollo at the zenith
shadows fall short
watch the shadows
keep watch how they tell
strong and stark when light is fierce
they can stab me but I cannot watch
over my shoulder
I do not look back
I walk on

صلاة الضّحى

تجعلُني أنظرُ بلهفةٍ للذي يأتي
على غير تخطيطٍ أو رغبةٍ منّي
ولكن، مهما تكن
هي لأجل ذلك حسنةٌ بالنسبة لي
حسنةٌ دون ريب
كل شيءٍ على طريق الرفاه
الطريق لكي أكون بخير.

صلاة الظهر

أرى إله الشمس في كبد السماء
عندما تسقطُ الخيالاتُ قصيرةً على الأرض
أراقبُها
أظلُّ أراقبُ ما الذي تقوله:
قويّةٌ وصلبةٌ في الضوء الشديد
لا أستطيع رؤيتهم من فوق كتفي عندما يطعنوني
فأنا لا أنظرُ إلى الخلف
فقط أتابعُ السيرَ إلى الأمامْ.

Midafternoon Prayer

Now is time to look back
to think about tomorrow
what must be done before night
food prepared for the needy
nurture, cleansing, stories, music, peace

Evening Prayer

'Now the day is over'
shadows slant deep and tall
a last long gleam of light
leaps on rock which transforms to
pearl or ruby
clouds stream in gold
to welcome the night
faithful stars in their courses
silence and sleep

صلاة العصر

إنّهُ وقت النظرِ للخلف الآن
والتفكير بالغد
وبالذي يجبُ فعله قبل هبوط الليل
تحضير الطعام للمحتاجين
التربية، التطهير، الحكايا، الموسيقا، السلام.

صلاة المساء

إنتهى اليومُ الآن
الخيالاتُ تتحدرُ طويلةً ومائلةً بحدّة
آخرُ شعاعٍ طويلٍ من الضوء
يقفزُ على الصخرة التي تتحوّلُ
إلى لؤلؤةٍ أو عقيق
الغيومُ تتدفّقُ مذهبّة
لتستقبل الليل بالترحاب
النجومُ المخلصةُ في مداراتها
صمتٌ ونَوَمْ.

Zakat (Almsgiving)

by Iyad Hayatleh
translated with Tessa Ransford

I will give lots of love
some money
keep a wee bit of money
and lots of love, my friends,
for the train of life to continue its journey.
I'll create an arena for poetry
on the threshing floor of my heart
and disperse its verses in all directions

You Dreamers,
Come let us share what the heavens grant
for we are tired of catching donations spilled from affluent
    people,
and starved stomachs are exhausted by sleeping hungry
and chewing the cud of crumbs.
Comrades of the road
Come share the love and forbearance
hunger and bread
the sweet and the bitter
the fear of crossroads and darkness

زكاة

إياد حياتله

سَأُعطي كثيراً مِنَ الحبِّ

بَعضاً مِنَ المال

أُبقي قَليلاً مِنَ المال

أيضاً، كثيراً مِنَ الحبَّ

كَيْ يستمرَّ بِنا يا رِفاقُ قطارُ الحياةْ

وأُنشئُ في بيدرِ القلبِ مَيدانَ شعرٍ

يُوزِّعُ أبياتَهُ في جميعِ الجِهاتْ

فَيا أيّها الحالمونَ هَلمّوا نَقاسَمُ ما قدْ تَهبْهُ السّماءُ

مَلَلنا مِنَ المُترفينَ اقتِناصَ الهِباتْ

وَمَلَّتْ بُطونُ الجِياعِ مَبيتَ الطّوى

وَاْجترارَ الفُتاتْ

رِفاقَ الطّريقِ

تَعالَوْا لِنَقتسِمَ الحبَّ والصبرَ

والجوعَ والخبزَ

والحلوَ والمرَّ

خَوفَ المفارقِ وَالحالكاتْ

Come let us baptise our hearts with sincerity,
for they have been rusted by flattering tyrants
and let us wash our souls in the springs of pure Zakat
before it is too late

Let us, with a life of few years
and of many poems and wishes
grapple the desolation of these paths

Come
there is still a bud of life on the horizon
flirting with our mornings despite these gloomy autumnal
    nights.
Let us ourselves go forward and weave a sun
for the blossom to cascade its perfume

Otherwise, sin will cast us in the cave of hibernation
and if we awoke
we would find what's gone has gone
and the dead have died
leaving only remnants of pictures
to overshadow the silent dust with sorrow –
and a fine thread of memories

تَعالَوْا – قُبَيْلَ فَواتِ الأوانِ –
نُعمّدُ بالحبَّ أفئدَةً صَدِئتْ من مديحِ الطّغاةْ
وَنَغسلُ أرواحَنا في ينابيعِ طُهرِ الزّكاةْ
نُصارعُ وَحشةَ هذي الدّروبِ بعمرٍ قصيرِ السّنينِ
كَثيرِ القصائدِ والأمنياتْ

تَعالَوْا
فَما زالَ في الأفقِ بُرعُمَةٌ مِنْ حَياةْ
تُغازلُ أصباحنا رغمَ ليلِ الخريفِ الكَئيبْ
فهيّا لِننسُجَ للزهرِ شمساً ليهدي إلينا نَوافيرَهُ العاطراتْ
وَإلاّ رَمتنا الخطايا بكهفِ السُّباتْ
فإمّا انتبهنا
وجدنا الّذي فاتَ فاتَ
وَمنْ ماتَ ماتْ
ولَمْ يَبقَ إلاّ بقايا رسومٍ
تُظلّلُ بالآهِ صمتَ الغبارِ
وَخيطٌ رَفيعٌ مِنَ الذكرياتْ.

Almsgiving

by Tessa Ransford

*The cost of a thing is the amount of 'life' we give to it,
that is required to be exchanged for it* (Thoreau)

Others have supported me
and I could not repay them
but give in my turn
give what I am
and share what I possess

The amount of life I give:
time, thought, intent
absorbed, devoured
is what it costs

زكاة

تيسّا رانسفورد
ترجمة إياد حياتله

(قيمةُ الشيء تُقاسُ بقيمة الحياة التي نمنحها له، وبقدرته التبادليّة) ثورو

ساعدني الآخرونْ
ولمْ أستطع أن أكافئهم على ذلكْ
ولكنّي بدوريَ أعطي
أعطي كينونتي
وأشارك ما أملكُ مع الآخرينْ

كميّةُ الحياة التي أمنحها
تُكلّفني، ما يُستهلكُ ويُلتهم
من الوقتِ والفكرةِ والنيّة

Yet life is not consumed
for the given is returned
in strength, not fully
but sufficient to continue
until the last is taken

So when I die I hope
this and that and he and she
will be endowed, as I have been
by this 'in person' charity

لكنّ الحياةَ كلّها لم تُستهلكْ بعد
فالذي يُعطى، يُردُّ بقوّةٍ،
ليسَ تماماً، ولكن بما يكفي للإستمرار
حتّى يُؤخذ الشيءَ الأخيرْ

لذلك، آملُ عندما أموت
هذا وذاك، هو وهي
أن ينذروا أنفسهم للصدقات
تماماً كما كنتُ أنا.

Siyam (Fasting)

by Iyad Hayatleh
translated with Tessa Ransford

From dawn to dusk
I go without food and water
and have no sense of hunger
for hunger is not the hunger of stomachs;
it is the longing
longing of lovers to be with their beloved;
it is the yearning
yearning of the homeless to return to the land
where memories for six decades
fall asleep on a promise,
the promised return of the dream
on the wings of the nightingale.

Years rush behind years
like clouds hiding days of deep grief
of exile
in waving layers
to leave only the evening of life
and tears of the stranger
with few remaining wishes.

O powerful night
please lift the veil of the sky
and bring glad tidings to the flood of worshippers,
to my family and my people,
tidings of the bright morning coming soon
with blessing for the whole world.

صيام

إياد حياتله

مِنَ الفجرِ حتّى الغروبِ
بِلا أكلَ لا ماءَ أمضي
ولستُ أحسُّ بجوعٍ، فما الجوعُ جوعُ البطونِ
ولكنّه الشوقُ، شوقُ الحبيبِ للقيا الحبيبِ
وتوقُ المشرّدِ نحو الرجوعِ لأرضٍ – لسِتِّ عقودٍ –
بِها الذكرياتُ على أهبةِ الوعدِ تغفو
وَترنو لِعودةِ حُلمٍ عَلى جانِحَيْ عَندليبِ

تمرُّ السّنونُ سراعاً وراءَ السّنينِ
غيوماً بطيّاتِها المائجاتِ تُخبّئُ

أيّامَ حزنِ المنافي الدّفينِ
ولا تُبقِ بالعمرِ إلاّ بُعيضَ الأماسي
وَما غلّفَ الدمعُ من أمنياتِ الغريبِ
فيا ليلة القدر هلاّ رفعتِ حجابَ السّماءِ قليلاً
وبشّرتِ سيلَ المصلّينَ، أهلي وناسي
بصبحٍ على العالمينَ مُنيرٍ
وخيرٍ كثيرٍ قريبِ

My love
my God, the Lord of heaven and earth
knower of things unseen
the affectionate, the merciful, the gracious, the greatest,
for you I fast my long day
to you I pray my solemn night.
May I win some approval from you
and may you remove from my shoulders the burden of sin.
Cleanse my soul for thirty days with the beauty of forbearance
and let me reach the day of Eid
a new person, with a new dress.

حَبيبي

إلهيَ ربُّ السّمواتِ والأرضِ .. علاّمُ كلِّ الغيوبِ

الودودُ الرحيمُ الرؤوفُ العظيمُ

إليكَ نهاري الطويل أصومُ

وليلي الطويل أقومُ

عساني أفوزُ ببعضٍ رضاكَ

وتَسقطَ عن كاهليَّ عظيمَ الذنوبِ

تُطهّرُ روحي بصبرٍ جميلٍ ثلاثينَ يوماً

لأفضي إلى العيدِ شخصا جديداً بثوبٍ قشيبِ.

Fasting

by Tessa Ransford

To go without food by choice is like
driving a car without fuel.
Is what matters the work to be done
or proving, improving ourselves?

Much harder for me
to give up working or caring,
to let go my longing to know,
to share, to love

You need to be needed
they say accusingly.
You always ask exactly what happened

I could forsake that need, that asking
only by force of will, by unwilling consent,
by continual heart-wrenching effort

صيام

تيسّا رانسفورد
ترجمة إياد حياتله

أن تمضي بدونِ طعامٍ طوعاً
كأنّك تقودُ سيّارة بدون وقود
الأهم، أن يُنجزَ العمل
أن نثبتَ، ونطوّرَ أنفسنا

الأكثرُ صعوبة بالنسبة لي
هو أن أتوقّفَ عن العملِ أو الرعاية
أن أفقدَ فضوليَ إلى المعرفة،
إلى المشاركة والحب

"أنتِ بحاجةٍ لأن تكونينَ مطلوبةً"
قالوا متّهمين:
"دائما، تستفهمين عن الذي حدث بالضبط"

أستطيعُ أن أتخلّى عن تلكَ الحاجة، عن ذلك السؤالْ
بقوّةِ الإرادة فقط، بالموافقة على مضض
بالجهدِ المتواصلِ الموجعِ للقلب.

Hajj (Pilgrimage)

by Iyad Hayatleh
translated with Tessa Ransford

Among an ocean of humanity I will surrender myself to Allah
and trace the steps of companions and followers
the steps of the noble honourable Prophet

My heart's love is for the ancient house;
my eyes travel to seek out Ibrahim, the father of the prophets,
and the boy who was to be sacrificed, saved by the ram from
    heaven
and Hagar, his mother, as she ran seven times in vain
before scooping the pure fresh water of Zamzam
for Ishmael to drink
and to quench our thirst through lifetimes of winters and
    summers

I travel into yesterday
through the miracles, Alkhaleel and Gabriel,
the black stone descended from heaven.
As I touch or kiss it my body trembles with devotion

حَجّ

إياد حياتله

سأسلمُ لله نفسيَ وسطَ بحورِ البشرْ
وأتبعُ خطوَ الصّحابةِ والتابعينَ
وَخطوَ النبيِّ الكريمِ الأغرّْ
لِبيتٍ عتيقٍ فؤاديَ يهوي
وَترحلُ عينايَ نَحوَ أبي الأنبياء
وَذاك الذبيحُ المفدّى بِكبشِ السّماء
وَهاجرُ تَسعى سِباعاً
وَتغرفُ من زمزم الماءَ عذباً زلالاً
لِتُسقى، وَنُسقى إلى آخرِ العمرِ حرّاً وَقرّْ

أسافرُ في الأمسِ
في المعجزاتِ، الخليلُ وجبريلُ
والحجرُ الأسودُ الْ جاءَ من جنّةِ اللهُ
إمّا لَمستُ وإمّا لثمتُ
ترى كلَّ جسميَ مِن وَرعٍ
إقشعَرّْ

On the mountain of Arafat I stand for long and cry out
raising my hands –
my senses tell the tale of my people:
My Lord, be merciful to refugees, to all human beings

I circumambulate the Ka'ba
and, Lord of the Worlds, my very being reverberates to your
    name
an echo which for centuries has been seeding this unplanted
    valley

Allah, who has no equal,
I am obedient to you.
To you the praise, the grace, the power!
We beseech you, for the sake of Mohammed, the Prophet of
    peace
to grant us a new dawn
even as the darkness is deepening

Peace be upon him sleeping in a patch of paradise.
How great he is above all other!

I return from the Hajj as a newborn child,
my heart choked with words.
When shall I enter you, Jerusalem, as a free man?
When will destiny answer the voice of the people?

عَلى عَرفاتَ طويلاً سأبكي
وأرفعُ كفّايَ، كلَّ الجوارحِ
قصّةَ شعبي سأحكي
إلهيَ رُحماكَ باللاجئينَ، بكلِّ البشرْ

أطوفُ وكُلُّ الخلايا بإسمكَ
يا سيّدَ العالمينَ تُردّدُ رَجعاً
قُروناً بوادٍ
بِدونِ زروعٍ هُناكَ استقَرْ

إلهيَ لَبّيكَ لا مِن شريكٍ لديكَ
لكَ الحمدُ والنِعمَةُ، المُلكُ لَكْ
فَهَبنا - إلهيَ - فجراً لأنّ الظلامَ حَلَكْ
بِجاهِ نبيِّ السّلامِ
سلامٌ عليهِ ينامُ بروضٍ
فَنِعمَ المقامُ ونِعمَ المقرْ

أعودُ مِنَ الحجِّ طفلاً جديداً
وَفي القلبِ غصَّ الكلامُ
متى أيّها القدسُ آتيكِ حُرّاً
متى يستجيبُ لِصوتِ الشعوبِ القدرْ!؟
متى يستجيبُ لِصوتِ الشعوبِ القدرْ!؟

Pilgrimage

by Tessa Ransford

I saw the Canterbury Pilgrims in procession,
tongues wagging with their tales,
a pellmell people's holiday excursion
along with dogs and horses, all and sundry there,
not sure they want to know each other well
but forced to get along the road together,
just that painted crowd, that April morning.

And so with me. I have no other chance
and need to make my journey from this place
this crowd of witnesses around me
this century and season
these rules and these conditions for the trip.

حَجّ

تيسّا رانسفورد
ترجمة إياد حياتله

رأيتُ حُجّاجَ كانتبري في موكبهمْ
تَتهادى ألسنتهم بالحكايا
أُناسٌ برحلتهم الفوضويّة
هناكَ، مع الكلابِ والخيولِ وكلّ اختلافاتهمْ
لستُ متأكّدةً إن كانوا سيتعرّفونَ على بعضهم جيّداً
لكنّهم أُجبروا على خوضِ غمارِ ذلك الطريق سويّةً
ذلكَ الحشدُ المرسومُ، في صباحٍ نيسانيّ.

وكذلكَ الأمرُ معي، لا أملكُ فرصةً أخرى
سوى الحاجةِ لبدء رحلتي من هذا المكان
بهذا الحشد الشاهد حولي
بهذا القرن، هذا الفصل
بهذه القواعد والشروط لهذه الرحلة.

As pilgrims we sleep after each day's advance
and shelter as best we may, no thought for the morrow
except to keep in the right direction. We jest and talk.
We have come far and must go forward each day
not waiting for what befalls. The temple dream
is granted to those who dare to wait
and wait in the dark
while, hardly discernible, an image lies ahead:
the great winged shrine to which we're all enthralled.

That shade of death is present in my childhood
disease and dynamite on either hand.
Progress does not describe my journey
winding round and each ordeal repeated:
Despond again, the *Hill* to climb, another and always another
with racket of fireworks, *Vanity Fair* recurring.

كَحجّاجٍ، ننامُ بعد شعائرِ كلّ يوم
ونهجعُ مفضّلينَ ألاّ نفكّر في الغد
عدا أن نواظبَ على السير بالإتجاه الصحيح، نمزحُ ونتحدث
حَقّقنا كثيراً، ويجبُ أن نمضي قُدماً كلّ يوم
غير منتظرينَ لما يحدث
معبد الحلم، يُمنحُ للذين يجرأونَ على الإنتظار
ولو كان انتظاراً في العتمة
بينما نحنُ بالكاد نميّزُ الصورة التي أمامنا:
الموتُ العظيم الذي يأسرنا جميعاً.

طيفُ الموتِ ما يزالُ حاضراً في طفولتي
المرضُ والديناميتُ في كلّ الجهات
التقدمُ لا يصفُ رحلتي
أطوفُ حولَ المحنِ التي تتكرر
اليأسُ مرّةً ثانيةً، تسلّق التلّة، دائما ودائماً
مع مضرب الألعاب الناريّة، ودار الغرور المتكررة.

When *Faithful* dies, as I let him, and *Hope*
scarcely abides without that friend;
when *Despair* imprisons
and *Promise* is no sure key of release,
I creep back and find old tales –
of love of love of love of love.
Not once in a lifetime this pilgrimage
but simply my life.

Now alone, yet in my own company,
I desire the delectable mountains
and wade through the river, yes,
hands outstretched to the children
without returning.

عندما يموتُ الإيمانُ، كما أريدُ أنا لهُ أن يفعل
نادراً ما يصمدُ الأملُ بدون صديقه ذلك
عندما يتحوّلُ اليأسُ إلى سجّان
ولا يكونُ الوعد مفتاحاً لحريّته
أزحفُ عائدةً للعثورِ على الحكاياتِ القديمة
حكايات الحبّ والحبّ والحبّ والحبّ والحب.
فهذا الحجُ ليس مرّةً بالعمر
بل هو حياتي كلّها.

وحيدةٌ الآن، بصحبةِ نفسي فقط
أطمحُ بالجبال اللذيذة
نعم،
وأن تمتدّ يداي دونَ رجوعٍ
لكلّ الأطفال.

Afterword

ARABIC POETRY IS still little known in the West. Yet poetry has always been the authentic Arab literary voice, from the days before Islam when the Bedouin nomads recited wonderfully complex and rich odes in praise of their tribe or lampooning their enemy, up to the modern era.

This beautifully entitled volume testifies to a vibrant tradition of poetry writing in Glasgow today. It provides a glimpse into the world view of a fine Palestinian poet living in exile from his homeland and it sheds light on how he and his well-known fellow-poet from Scotland have forged a path together towards a better understanding of each other's religious traditions and culture, not by debate, but through the medium of poetry and translating or co-translating each other's work.

The depiction of this book as a rug is most felicitous; indeed its eleven poems have multiple interwoven strands, including the theme of the diasporic Palestinian people, yearning for their homeland, and extended meditations by both poets on the spiritual dimensions underlying the five pillars of Islam – the profession of faith, prayer, fasting, almsgiving and pilgrimage. The poems in this volume are about ritual actions through which Muslims respond to their faith. They unite the worldwide community of well over a billion Muslims. Let me briefly comment on two of these pillars, prayer and pilgrimage. The communal nature of prayer, performed in a strictly timed sequence of movements, strengthens feelings of solidarity. They are the same in Glasgow as they are in Jerusalem, Jakarta or Dakar. So too, at a human level, performing the shared rites of pilgrimage in Mecca is an act of reinforcement: the unity of all believers is palpably demonstrated. Yet the performance of the five pillars is not merely an external matter; to be acceptable to God, they have to spring from right intention, from the heart.

خاتمة

كارول هيلينبراند
أستاذة فخريّة في التاريخ الإسلامي
جامعة أدنبرة
ترجمة إياد حياتله

سجّادة من ألف لون

مع أنّ الشعر قد شكّل دائماً الصوت الحقيقي للأدب العربي، منذ أيّام ما قبل الإسلام عندما كان البدو الرحّل يرتّلون بروعةٍ قصائدهم الغنيّة المركّبة في مدح قبائلهم وهجاء القبائل الأخرى، حتّى العصر الحديث. إلاّ أنّ الشعر العربي لا يزال غير معروفٍ كثيراً في الغرب.

هذا الكتاب ذو العنوان الجميل "سجّادةٌ من ألف لون"، يشهد على التقاليد الحيويّة للكتابة الشعريّة في غلاسكو اليوم، ويعطي لمحةً عن منظر عالم شاعرٍ فلسطينيّ رائع يعيشُ منفيّاً عن وطنه، ملقياً الضوء على كيف أنّه وزميلته الشاعرة الأسكوتلنديّة المعروفة قد أقاما مساراً مشتركاً من أجل فهمٍ أفضل للتقاليد الدينيّة وثقافة كلٍّ منهما، ليس عن طريق المناقشة، ولكن من خلال الشعر والترجمة، أو الترجمة التشاركيّة لأعمال بعضهما البعض.

وصف هذا الكتاب بالسجّادة كان موفّقاً جدّاً، لأنّه حقيقةً يتألّف من إحدى عشرة قصيدة تتشابك في خيوطٍ متعدّدة، بما فيها موضوع شتات الشعب الفلسطيني وحنينه إلى وطنه، والتأمّلات الموسّعة للشاعرين في الأبعاد الروحيّة المؤسّسة لأركان الإسلام الخمسة، الجهر بالإيمان، الصلاة، الصيام، الزكاة، والحج. وتتمحور قصائد هذا الكتاب حول الشعائر التي يستجيب المسلمون من خلال تطبيقها لدينهم، والتي يتوحد حولها أكثر من مليار مسلم يشكّلون مجتمعاً واحداً على امتداد العالم.

إسمحوا لي أن أعلّق بإيجازٍ على اثنين من هذه الأركان، الصلاة والحج، الجوهر البسيط للصلاة هو أنّها تؤدّى في تسلسل حركاتٍ دقيق التوقيت يقوّي مشاعر التضامن، إنّها نفسها في غلاسكو أو القدس، جاكرتا أو داكار. وأيضاً على المستوى الإنساني، إنّ تعزيز وحدة المؤمنين يتجلّى وبشكل ملموسٍ من خلال تأدية مناسك الحج المشتركة في مكّة. ومع هذا فإنّ ممارسة أركان الإسلام الخمسة ليست مجرّد مسألة خارجيّة، ولكنّها يجب أن تنبع من النيّة الصافية، من القلب، لتحظى بقبولٍ من الله.

The Qur'an has always exerted a deep influence on Arabic literature in a way similar to the profound inspiration of the 1611 King James Bible for writers in English-speaking countries. In his poem on prayer, Hayatleh mentions Chapter 1 – the Fatiha (the Opening) – which is especially beloved of Muslims. It is the veritable essence of Islamic belief, being the foundation of every prayer, and it is recited in the mourning and memory of the dead. He mentions the two testimonies (the Shahada) as well, which is breathed into the ear of a baby at birth, and into the ear of one at the point of death. Similarly, the New Testament resonates in Ransford's poems, as do allusions to Bunyan, Milton, Chaucer and Julian of Norwich. This deeply embedded substratum of echoes of the Muslim and Christian faiths in both sets of poems adds parallelism and overarching unity to this noble project.

In many ways the verses in this book fit into the mystical poetic traditions of both Muslims and Christians. Certain Qur'anic verses are couched in mysterious and richly symbolic verse. A very famous example is the so-called 'Light Verse' (chapter 24, verse 35) that is so beloved of the Sufis and part of which Hayatleh quotes in his poem on fasting. Moreover, Ransford's poem on prayer also focuses on the importance of light, symbolised as the 'daystar' in her heart. As for the pilgrimage (*hajj*), it involves the most important earthly journey in the lives of Muslims. They go, 'swayed', as the great Muslim traveller Ibn Battuta so eloquently put it, 'by an overmastering impulse within me'. And the pilgrimage is a life-changing experience. At a more profound level, the journey to the Ka'ba and their experiences there enable believers to become a conduit of sacred power, able to transmit the blessings of Mecca to their fellow-Muslims in the many distant countries from which they have come. Ransford's poem on pilgrimage extends the metaphor of this earthly journey to embrace the image of the human life from the cradle to the grave.

لطالما مارس القرآن تأثيراً عميقاً في الأدب العربي، بطريقة مشابهة للإلهام العميق لإنجيل الملك جيمس 1611 على الكتّاب في البلدان الناطقة بالإنكليزيّة. في قصيدته عن الصلاة، يذكر "حياتله" السّورة الأولى من القرآن "الفاتحة" المحبّبة للمسلمين بشكل خاص، إنّها الجوهر الحقيقيّ للعقيدة الإسلاميّة كونها أساس كل صلاة، كما أنّها تُتلى في تأبين وذكرى الأموات. كما يُشير الشاعر إلى الشهادتين اللتين تُهمسان من ضمن الأذان في أذن المولود المسلم لحظة ولادته، وأيضاً إبان إحتضار أي مسلم. وبالمثل فإنّ صدى العهد الجديد يتردد في قصائد "رانسفورد" عندما تلمّح إلى بنيان، ميلتون، تشوسر، وجوليان "راهبة نورويتش". إنّ الأصداء العميقة للأسس المتينة للدياتتين الإسلاميّة و المسيحيّة في مجموعتي القصائد تضيفُ توازياً ووحدةً جامعةً لهذا المشروع النبيل.

في نواحٍ كثيرة من هذا الكتاب، تتناسب أشعاره بشكل جميل مع التقاليد الشعريّة الصوفيّة للمسلمين والمسيحيين على حدٍّ سواء، فقد ضُمّنت بعض الآيات القرآنية في أبيات شعريّة غنيّة بالرمزيّة المبهمة، وكأشهر مثال على ذلك سورة النّور، (السّورة 24، الآية 35) والتي تحظى بحبٍّ شديدٍ لدى المتصوّفة، والتي اقتبس "حياتله" جزءاً منها في قصيدته عن الصيام. علاوةً على ذلك، تركّز قصيدة "رانسفورد" الجميلة عن الصلاة على أهميّة الضوء، رامزةً له كالشمس في قلبها.

أمّا الحج الذي يشتمل على أهم رحلة دنيوية للمسلمين المؤتمرين بأمر الله، كما ترجم ذلك ببلاغة الرحّالة الإسلاميّ الكبير "إبن بطّوطة": "بقوّة الإندفاع المسيطر في داخلي". فـإنّه تجربـة مغيّـرة للحياة. على مستوىً أكثر عمقاً، لإنّ تجربة المؤمنين في رحلتهم إلى الكعبة تمكّنهم من أن يصبحوا وسيلة لنقل القوّة المقدّسة، القادرة على بثّ بركات مكّة إلى إخوانهم المسلمين في بلادٍ شتّى بعيـدةٍ عن التي جاؤوا هم منها. وبالمقابل نجد أنّ قصيدة "رانسفورد" عن الحج تستخدم جماليّة المجاز في توسيع هذه الرحلة الأرضيّة لتشمل صورة حياة الإنسان من المهد إلى اللحد.

In sum, therefore, these poems reach out to everyone beyond the confines of particular communities and religious backgrounds. Here is a coming together of faith, experience and shared humanity from both sides of a religious divide.

Carole Hillenbrand
Professor Emerita of Islamic History
University of Edinburgh

وبالتالي، في خلاصة القول، إنّ هذه القصائد تستطيع أن تصل إلى الجميع بغضّ النظر عن خصوصيّة بعض المجتمعات والخلفيّات الدينيّة. هنا يكمنُ الإلتقاء الجميل للإيمان، والتجربة والإنسانيّة التشاركيّة لِكلا جانبي التوزّع الديني.

Luath Press Limited
committed to publishing well written books worth reading

LUATH PRESS takes its name from Robert Burns, whose little collie Luath (*Gael.*, swift or nimble) tripped up Jean Armour at a wedding and gave him the chance to speak to the woman who was to be his wife and the abiding love of his life. Burns called one of 'The Twa Dogs' Luath after Cuchullin's hunting dog in Ossian's *Fingal*. Luath Press was established in 1981 in the heart of Burns country, and is now based a few steps up the road from Burns' first lodgings on Edinburgh's Royal Mile.

Luath offers you distinctive writing with a hint of unexpected pleasures.

Most bookshops in the UK, the US, Canada, Australia, New Zealand and parts of Europe either carry our books in stock or can order them for you. To order direct from us, please send a £sterling cheque, postal order, international money order or your credit card details (number, address of cardholder and expiry date) to us at the address below. Please add post and packing as follows: UK – £1.00 per delivery address; overseas surface mail – £2.50 per delivery address; overseas airmail – £3.50 for the first book to each delivery address, plus £1.00 for each additional book by airmail to the same address. If your order is a gift, we will happily enclose your card or message at no extra charge.

Luath Press Limited
543/2 Castlehill
The Royal Mile
Edinburgh EH1 2ND
Scotland

Telephone: 0131 225 4326 (24 hours)
email: sales@luath.co.uk
Website: www.luath.co.uk